I0818944

OPINION

OF

ATTORNEY GENERAL BATES

ON

CITIZENSHIP.

WASHINGTON:
GOVERNMENT PRINTING OFFICE.
1863.

OPINION.

Attorney General's Office,
November 29, 1862.

Hon. S. P. Chase,
Secretary of the Treasury.

Sir: Some time ago I had the honor to receive your letter submitting, for my opinion, the question whether or not *colored men* can be citizens of the United States. The urgency of other unavoidable engagements, and the great importance of the question itself, have caused me to delay the answer until now.

Your letter states that "the schooner Elizabeth and Margaret, of New Brunswick, is detained by the revenue cutter Tiger, at South Amboy, New Jersey, because commanded by a 'colored man,' and so by a person not a citizen of the United States. As colored masters are numerous in our coasting trade, I submit, for your opinion, the question suggested by Captain Martin, of the Tiger: *Are colored men citizens* of the United States, and therefore competent to command American vessels?"

The question would have been more clearly stated if, instead of saying *are colored men citizens*, it had been said, *can colored men be citizens of the United States;* for within our borders and upon our ships, both of war and commerce, there may be *colored* men, and *white* men, also, who are not citizens of the United States. In treating the subject, I shall endeavor to answer your question as if it imported only this: Is a man legally incapacitated to be a citizen of the United States by the sole fact that he is a *colored*, and not a white man?

Who is a citizen? What constitutes a citizen of the United States? I have often been pained by the fruitless search in our law books and the records of our courts, for a clear and satisfactory definition of the phrase *citizen of the United States.* I find no such definition, no authoritative establishment of the meaning of the phrase, neither by a course of judicial decisions in our courts, nor by the continued and consentaneous action of the different branches of our political government. For aught I see to the contrary, the subject is now as little understood in its details and elements, and the question as open to argument and to speculative criticism, as it was at the beginning of the government. Eighty years of practical enjoyment of citizenship, under the Constitution, have not sufficed to teach us either the exact meaning of the word, or the constituent elements of the thing we prize so highly.

In most instances, within my knowledge, in which the matter of citizenship has been discussed, the argument has not turned upon the existence and the intrinsic qualities of citizenship itself, but upon the claim of some right or privilege as belonging to and inhering in the character of citizen. In this way we are easily led into errors both of fact and principle. We see individuals, who are known to be citizens, in the actual enjoyment of certain rights and privileges, and in the actual exercise of certain powers, social and political, and we, inconsiderately, and without any regard to legal and logical consequences, attribute to those individuals, and to all of their class, the enjoyment of those rights and privileges and the exercise of those powers as incidents to their citizenship, and belonging to them only in their quality of citizens.

In such cases it often happens that the rights enjoyed and the powers exercised have no relation whatever to the quality of citizen, and might be as perfectly enjoyed and exercised by known aliens. For instance, General Bernard, a distinguished soldier and devoted citizen of France, for a long time filled the office of general of engineers in the service of the United States, all the time avowing his French allegiance, and, in fact, closing his relations with the United States by resigning his commission and returning to the service of his own native country. This, and all such instances, (and they are many,) go to prove that in this country the legal capacity to hold office is not confined to citizens, and therefore that the fact of holding any office for which citizenship is not specially prescribed by law as a qualification, is no proof that the incumbent is an American citizen.

Again, with regard to the right of suffrage, that is, the right to choose officers of government, there is a very common error to the effect that the right to vote for public officers is one of the constituent elements of American citizenship, the leading faculty indeed of the citizen, the test at once of his legal right, and the sufficient proof of his membership of the body politic. No error can be greater than this, and few more injurious to the right understanding of our constitutions and the actual working of our political governments. It is not only not true in law or in fact, in principle or in practice, but the reverse is conspicuously true; for I make bold to affirm that, viewing the nation as a whole, or viewing the States separately, there is no district in the nation in which a majority of the known and recognized citizens are not excluded by law from the right of suffrage. Besides those who are excluded specially on account of some personal defect, such as paupers, idiots, lunatics, and men convicted of infamous crimes, and, in some States, soldiers, all females and all minor males are also excluded. And these, in every community, make the majority; and yet, I think, no one will venture to deny that women and children, and lunatics, and even convict felons, may be citizens of the United States.

Our code (unlike the codes of France, and perhaps some other nations) makes no provision for loss or legal deprivation of citizenship. Once a citizen, (whether *natus* or *datus*, as Sir Edward Coke expresses it,) always a citizen, unless changed by the volition and act of the individual. Neither infancy nor madness nor crime can take away from the subject the quality of citizen. And our laws do, in express terms, declare women and children to be citizens. See, for one instance, the act of Congress of February 10, 1855, 10 Stat., 604.

The Constitution of the United States does not declare who are and who are not citizens, nor does it attempt to describe the constituent elements of citizenship. It leaves that quality where it found it, resting upon the fact of home-birth, and upon the laws of the several States. Even in the important matter of electing members of Congress, it does no more than provide that "the House of Representatives shall be composed of members chosen every second year *by the people* of the several States; and the *electors* in the several States shall have the qualifications requisite for the electors of the most numerous branch of the State legislature." Here the word *citizen* is not mentioned, and it is a legal fact, known of course to all lawyers and publicists, that the constitutions of several of the States, in specifying the qualifications of electors, do altogether omit and exclude the word *citizen* and *citizenship.* I will refer, in proof, to but three instances:

1. The constitution of Massachusetts, adopted in 1779–'80, in article 4 of section 3, chapter 1, provides as follows: "Every *male person* (being twenty-one years of age, and *resident* of a particular town in this commonwealth for the space of one year next preceding) having a freehold estate within the same town of the annual income of three pounds, or any estate of the value of sixty pounds, shall have the

right to vote in the choice of representative or representatives for said town."

2. The constitution of North Carolina, adopted in 1776, after a bill of rights, and after reciting that "whereas allegiance and protection are, in their nature, reciprocal, and the one should of right be refused when the other is withdrawn," declares, in section 8, "that all *freemen* at the age of twenty-one years, who have been *inhabitants* of any one county within the State twelve months immediately preceding the day of any election, and shall have paid public taxes, shall be entitled to vote for members of the house of commons for the county in which he resides."

3. The constitution of Illinois, adopted in 1818, in article 2, section 27, declares that "in all elections all *white male inhabitants* above the age of twenty-one years, having resided in the State six months next preceding the election, shall enjoy the right of an elector; but no person shall be entitled to vote except in the county or district in which he shall actually reside at the time of the election."

These three constitutions belong to States widely separated in geographical position, varying greatly from each other in habits, manners, and pursuits, having different climates, soils, productions, and domestic institutions; and yet not one of the three has made *citizenship* a necessary qualification for a voter; all three of them exclude all females, but only one of them (Illinois) has excluded the black man from the right of suffrage. And it is historically true that the practice has conformed to the theory of those constitutions, respectively; for, without regard to citizenship, the colored man has not voted in Illinois, and freemen of all colors have voted in North Carolina and Massachusetts.

From all this it is manifest that American citizenship does not necessarily depend upon nor coexist with the legal capacity to hold office and the right of suffrage, either or both of them. The Constitution of the United States, as I have said, does not define citizenship; neither does it declare who may vote, nor who may hold office, except in regard to a few of the highest national functionaries. And the several States, as far as I know, in exercising that power, act independently and without any controlling authority over them, and hence it follows that there is no limit to their power in that particular but their own prudence and discretion; and therefore we are not surprised to find that these faculties of voting and holding office are not uniform in the different States, but are made to depend upon a variety of facts, purely discretionary, such as age, sex, race, color, property, residence in a particular place, and length of residence there.

On this point, then, I conclude that no person in the United States did ever exercise the right of suffrage in virtue of the naked, unassisted fact of citizenship. In every instance the right depends upon some additional fact and cumulative qualification, which may as perfectly exist without as with citizenship.

I am aware that some of our most learned lawyers and able writers have allowed themselves to speak upon this subject in loose and indeterminate language. They speak of "all the rights, privileges, and immunities guaranteed by the Constitution to the citizen" without telling us what they are. They speak of a man's citizenship as defective and imperfect, because he is supposed not to have "all the civil rights," (all the *jura civitatis*, as expressed by one of my predecessors,) without telling what particular rights they are nor what relation they have, if any, with citizenship. And they suggest, without affirming, that there may be different grades of citizenship of higher and lower degree in point of legal virtue and efficacy; one grade "in the sense of the Constitution," and another inferior grade made by a State and not recognized by the Constitution.

In my opinion the Constitution uses the word citizen only to express the political quality of the individual in his relations to the nation; to declare that he is a member of the body politic, and bound to it by the reciprocal obligation of allegiance on the one side and protection on the other. And I have no knowledge of any other kind of political citizenship, higher or lower, statal or national; or of any other sense in which the word has been used in the Constitution, or can be used properly in the laws of the United States. The phrase "a citizen of the United States," without addition or qualification, means neither more nor less than a member of the nation. And all such are, politically and legally, equal—the child in the cradle and its father in the Senate are equally citizens of the United States. And its need no argument to prove that every citizen of a State is, necessarily, a citizen of the United States; and to me it is equally clear that every citizen of the United States is a citizen of the particular State in which he is domiciled.

And as to voting and holding office, as that privilege is not essential to citizenship, so the deprivation of it by law is not a deprivation of citizenship. No more so in the case of a negro than in case of a white woman or child.

In common speech the word citizen, with more or less of truth and pertinency, has a variety of meanings. Sometimes it is used in contrast with *soldier;* sometimes with *farmer* or *countryman;* sometimes with *alien* or *foreigner.* Speaking of a particular man we ask, Is he a citizen or a soldier? meaning, is he engaged in civil or military pursuits? Is he a citizen or a countryman? meaning, does he live in the city or in the country? Is he a citizen or an alien? meaning, is he a member of our body politic or of some other nation? The first two predicates relate only to the pursuits and to the place of abode of the person. The last is always and wholly political, and concerns only the political and governmental relations of the individual. And it is only in this last sense, the political, that the word is ever used in the Constitution and statutes of the United States.

We have *natural-born* citizens, (Constitution, article 2, 5,) not made by law or otherwise, but *born.* And this class is the large majority; in fact, the mass of our citizens; for all others are exceptions specially provided for by law. As they became citizens in the natural way, *by birth,* so they remain citizens during their natural lives, unless, by their own voluntary act, they expatriate themselves and become citizens or subjects of another nation. For we have no law (as the French have) to *decitizenize* a citizen, who has become such either by the natural process of birth, or by the legal process of adoption. And in this connection the Constitution says not one word, and furnishes not one hint, in relation to the color or to the ancestral race of the "natural-born citizen." Whatever may have been said, in the opinion of judges and lawyers, and in State statutes, about negroes, mulattoes, and persons of color, the Constitution is wholly silent upon that subject. The Constitution itself does not *make* the citizens, (it is, in fact, made by them.) It only intends and recognizes such of them as are natural—home-born—and provides for the *naturalization* of such of them as were alien—foreign-born—making the latter, as far as nature will allow, like the former.

And I am not aware of any provision in our laws to warrant us in presuming the existence in this country, of a class of persons intermediate between citizens and aliens. In England there is such a class, clearly defined by law, and called *denizens.* "A denizen (says Sir William Blackstone) is an *alien born,* but who has obtained, *ex donatione regis,* letters patent to make him an English subject; a high and incommunicable branch of the *royal prerogative.* A denizen is in a kind of middle state between an alien and a natural-born subject, and partakes of both of them." (I *Sharswood's Bl. Com.*, 374.) In this country I know of but one legal authority tending to show the existence of such a class among us. One of my learned predecessors, Mr. Legaré, (4 *Opin.*, 147,) supposes that there may be such a class, and that free colored persons may be ranked in it. Yet, in that same opinion, he declares that a "free man of color, a *native* of this country, may be admitted to the privileges of a pre-emptioner under the 10th section of the act of the 4th September, 1841." And that act declares that a pre-emptioner must be either a citizen of the United States or a person who had declared his intention to become a citizen, as required by the naturalization laws. Of course, the "colored man" must have been a *citizen* or he could not have entered the land under that act of Congress. If not a citizen *then*, by virtue of his native birth, he never could become one by force of law. For our laws extend the privileges of naturalization to such persons only as are "*aliens*, being free *white* persons," and he was neither; not alien, because natural-born in the country, and not a free *white* person, because, though free, confessedly "a man of color."

It occurs to me that the discussion of this great subject of national citizenship has been much embarrassed and obscured by the fact that it is beset with artificial difficulties, extrinsic to its nature, and having little or no relation to its great political and national characteristics. And these difficulties, it seems to me, flow mainly from two sources: First, the existence among us of a large class of people whose physical qualities visibly distinguish them from the mass of our people, and mark a different race, and who, for the most part, are held in bondage. This visible difference and servile connection present difficulties hard to be conquered; for they unavoidably lead to a more complicated system of government, both legislative and administrative, than would be required if all our people were of one race, and undistinguishable by outward signs. And this, without counting the effect upon the opinions, passions, and prejudices of men. Second, the common habit of many of our best and most learned men (the wise aptitude of which I have not been able to perceive) of testing the political status and governmental relation of our people by standards drawn from the laws and history of ancient Greece and Rome, without, as I think, taking sufficient account of the organic differences between their governments and ours.

A very learned writer upon the Politics of Greece (Heeren, Bancroft's translation, p. 105) informs us "that the essential character of the new political form assumed by Greece consisted in the circumstance that the free States which were formed were *nothing but cities* with their districts; and their constitutions were, consequently, only *forms of city governments.* This point of view (the learned author warns us) must never be lost sight of."

And the wise observation of the author applies to Italy as well; for the earliest free cities of Italy were but Grecian colonies, which (bringing along with them the higher civilization of their parent country, and its better notions of civil polity) by degrees diffused the light of knowledge, and consequently the love of liberty among the then barbarous people of the Italian peninsula. The Italians, profiting by the good example, founded cities of their own upon the Grecian models, and each new Italian city became an independent State. How long this condition of things continued I know not; but it continued until Rome outgrew all the neighboring communities, and subdued them all (the Grecian colonies included) under its power. Still *the city* ruled, and from time to time granted to such as it would (and withheld from such as it would) the title of *Roman*, and the rights of Roman citizens.

In process of time, when the dominant power of Rome had expanded over Greece and western Asia, the same civil polity was still continued. As it had been in Italy, so it was in Greece and Asia. In the countries and kingdoms subdued by the Roman arms and transformed into Roman provinces, the same system of government still prevailed. Rome, by her pro-consuls and other governors, ruled the conquered nations with absolute sway. And the ruling power at Rome, whether republican or imperial, granted, from time to time, to communities and to individuals in the conquered east the title of *Roman* and the rights of Roman citizens.

A striking example of this Roman naturalization, of its controlling authority as a political law, and of its beneficent power to protect a persecuted citizen, may be found in the case of St. Paul, as it is graphically reported in the Acts of the Apostles. Paul, being at Jerusalem, was in great peril of his life from his own countrymen, the Jews, who accused him of crimes against their own law and faith, and were about to put him to death by mob violence, when he was rescued by the commander of the Roman troops and taken into a fort for security. He first explained, both to the Roman officer and to

his own countrymen, who were clamoring against him, his local status and municipal relations, that he was a Jew of Tarsus, a *natural-born citizen* of no mean city, and that he had been brought up in Jerusalem in the strictest manner according to the law and faith of the fathers. But this did not appease the angry crowd, who were proceeding with great violence to kill him. And then "the chief captain commanded that he be brought into the castle, and bade that he should be *examined by scourging*," (that is, tortured to enforce confession.) "And as they bound him with thongs, Paul said unto the centurion that stood by, Is it lawful for you to scourge a man that is *a Roman and uncondemned?* When the centurion heard *that* he went out and told the chief captain, saying, Take heed what thou doest, *for this man is a Roman.* Then the chief captain came and said, Tell me, art thou a *Roman?* He said Yea, and the chief captain said, With a great sum obtained I *this freedom.* And Paul said, But I was *free born.* Then straightway *they* departed from him which should have *examined* him. And the chief captain also was *afraid*, after he knew that he was a *Roman*, and because he had *bound him.*"

Thus Paul, under circumstances of great danger and obloquy, asserted his immunity, as "a Roman uncondemned," from ignominious constraint and cruel punishment, a constraint and punishment against which, as a mere provincial subject of Rome, he had no legal protection. And thus the Roman officers instantly, and with fear, obeyed the law of their country and respected the sacred franchise of the Roman citizen.

Paul, as we know by this record, was a natural-born citizen of Tarsus, and as such, no doubt, had the municipal freedom of that city; but that would not have protected him against the thongs and the lash. How he became a *Roman* we learn from other historical sources. Cæsar granted to the people of Tarsus (for some good service done, probably for taking his side in the war which resulted in the establishment of the empire) the title of *Roman*, and the freedom of Roman citizens. And, considering the chronology of events, this grant must have been older than Paul; and therefore he truly said *I was free born*—a free citizen of Rome, and as such exempt by law from degrading punishment.

And this immunity did not fill the measure of his rights as a citizen. As a Roman, it was his right to be tried by the supreme authority, at the capital of the empire. And when he claimed that right, and appealed from the jurisdiction of the provincial governor to the emperor at Rome, his appeal was instantly allowed, and he was remitted to "Cæsar's judgment."

I have dwelt the longer upon this case of Paul, because it is a *leading case* in Roman jurisprudence in the matter of the "*jus Romanum.*" And in so far as there is any analogy between Roman and American citizenship, it is strictly applicable to us. Its authenticity is unquestionable, and by its lucid statement of facts in minute detail leaves no room to doubt the legal merits of the case. It establishes the great *protective rights* of the citizen, but, like our own national constitution, it is silent about his *powers*. It protected Paul against oppression and outrage, but said nothing about his right of suffrage or his eligibility to office.

As far as I know, Mr. Secretary, you and I have no better title to the citizenship which we enjoy than the "accident of birth"—the fact that we happened to be born in the United States. And our Constitution, in speaking of *natural-born citizens*, uses no affirmative language to make them such, but only recognizes and reaffirms the universal principle, common to all nations, and as old as political society, that the people born in a country do constitute the nation, and, as individuals, are *natural* members of the body politic.

If this be a true principle, and I do not doubt it, it follows that every person born in the country is, at the moment of birth, *prima facie* a citizen; and he who would deny it must take upon himself the burden of proving some great disfranchisement strong enough to override the "*natural-born*" right as recognized by the Constitution in terms the most simple and comprehensive, and without any reference to race or color, or any other accidental circumstance.

That *nativity* furnishes the rule, both of duty and of right as between the individual and the government, is a historical and political truth so old and so universally accepted that it is needless to prove it by authority. Nevertheless, for the satisfaction of those who may have doubts upon the subject, I note a few books, which, I think, cannot fail to remove all such doubts—Kent's Com., vol. 2, part 4, sec. 25; Bl. Com., book 1, ch. 10, p. 365; 7 Co. Rep., Calvin's case; 4 Term Rep., p. 300, Doe *v.* Jones; 3 Pet. Rep., p. 246; Shanks *v.* Dupont; and see a very learned treatise, attributed to Mr. Binney, in 2 Am. Law Reporter, 193.

In every civilized country the individual is *born* to duties and rights—the duty of allegiance and the right to protection; and these are correlative obligations, the one the price of the other, and they constitute the all-sufficient bond of union between the individual and his country; and the country he is born in *is*, *prima facie*, *his* country. In most countries the old law was broadly laid down that this natural connection between the individual and his native country was perpetual; at least, that the tie was indissoluble by the act of the subject alone.—(See Bl. Com. *supra;* 3 Pet. Rep. *supra.*)

But that law of the perpetuity of allegiance is now changed, both in Europe and America. In some countries by silent acquiescence, in others by affirmative legislation. In England, while asserting the perpetuity of natural allegiance, the King, for centuries past, has exercised the power to grant letters of denization to foreigners, making them English subjects, and the Parliament has exercised at pleasure the power of naturalization.

In France the whole subject is regulated by written law, which plainly declares who are citizens (*citoyens Français*) and who are only *the French*, (*Français*,) meaning the whole body of the French people.—(See *Les Codes Français, titre premier.*) And the same law distinctly sets forth by what means citzenship and the quality of *French* may be lost and regained; and maintains fully the right of expatriation in the subject, and the power of naturalization in the nation to which he goes.

In the United States it is too late now to deny the political rights and obligations conferred and imposed by nativity; for our laws do not pretend to create or enact them, but do assume and recognize them as things known to all men, because pre-existent and natural; and therefore things of which the laws must take cognizance. Acting out this guiding thought, our Constitution does no more than grant to Congress (rather than to any other department) the power "to establish a *uniform rule* of naturalization." And our laws made in pursuance thereof indue the *made* citizen with all the rights and obligations of the *natural* citizen. And so strongly was Congress impressed with the great legal fact that the child takes its political status in the nation where it is born, that it was found necessary to pass a law to prevent the *alienage* of children of our known fellow-citizens who happen to be born in foreign countries. The act of February 10, 1852, 10 Statutes, 604, provides that "persons," (not *white* persons,) "persons heretofore born, or hereafter to be born, out of the limits and jurisdiction of the United States, whose fathers were or shall be, at the time of their birth, citizens of the United

States, shall be deemed and considered, and are hereby declared to be, citizens of the United States: *Provided, however*, That the rights of citizenship shall not descend to persons whose fathers never resided in the United States.

"SEC. 2. *And be it further enacted*, That any woman who might lawfully be naturalized under the existing laws, married, or who shall be married to a citizen of the United States, shall be deemed and taken to be a citizen."

But for that act, children of our citizens who happen to be born at London, Paris, or Rome, while their parents are there on a private visit of pleasure or business, might be brought to the native home of their parents, only to find that they themselves were aliens in their father's country, incapable of inheriting their father's land, and with no right to demand the protection of their father's government.

That is the law of birth at the common law of England, clear and unqualified; and now, both in England and America, modified only by statutes, made from time to time, to meet emergencies as they arise.

I have said that, *prima facie*, every person in this country is born a citizen; and that he who denies it in individual cases assumes the burden of stating the exception to the general rule, and proving the fact which works the disfranchisement. There are but a few exceptions commonly made and urged as disqualifying facts. I lay no stress upon the small and admitted class of the *natural-born* composed of the children of foreign ministers and the like; and

1. *Slavery*, and whether or no it is legally possible for a slave to be a citizen. On that point I make no question, because it is not within the scope of your enquiry, and does not concern the person to whom your enquiry relates.

2. *Color*.—It is strenuously insisted by some that "persons of color," though born in the country, are not capable of being citizens of the United States. As far as the Constitution is concerned, this is a naked assumption; for the Constitution contains not one word upon the subject. The exclusion, if it exist, must then rest upon some fundamental fact which, in the reason and nature of things, is so inconsistent with citizenship that the two cannot coexist in the same person. Is mere *color* such a fact? Let those who assert it prove that it is so. It has never been so understood nor put into practice in the nation from which we derive our language, laws, and institutions, and our very morals and modes of thought; and, as far

He does not discuss the question whether a slave can be a citizen, as that was as I know, there is not a single nation in Christendom which does not regard the new-found idea with incredulity, if not disgust. What can there be in the mere *color* of a man (we are speaking now not of *race*, but of *color* only) to disqualify him for bearing true and faithful allegiance to his native country, and for demanding the protection of that country? And these two, allegiance and protection, constitute the sum of the duties and rights of a "natural-born citizen of the United States."

3. *Race.*—There are some who, abandoning the untenable objection of *color*, still contend that no person descended from *negroes of the African race* can be a citizen of the United States. Here the objection is not *color* but *race* only. The individual objected to may be of very long descent from African negroes, and may be as white as leprosy, or as the intermixture for many generations with the Caucasian race can make him; still, if he can be traced back to *negroes of the African race*, he cannot, they say, be a citizen of the United States! And why not? The Constitution certainly does not forbid it, but is silent about *race* as it is about *color*.

Our nationality was created and our political government exists by written law, and inasmuch as that law does not exclude persons of that descent, and as its terms are manifestly broad enough to include them, it follows inevitably that such persons, born in the country, must be citizens, unless the fact of African descent be so incompatible with the fact of citizenship that the two cannot exist together. If they can coexist, in nature and reason, then they do coexist in persons of the indicated class, for there is no law to the contrary. I am not able to perceive any antagonism, legal or natural, between the two facts.

But it is said that African negroes are a degraded race, and that all who are tainted with that degradation are forever disqualified for the functions of citizenship. I can hardly comprehend the thought of the absolute incompatibility of degradation and citizenship. I thought that they often went together. But if it be true with regard to races, it seems to me more cogently true with regard to individuals. And if I be right in this, there are many sorrowful examples in the legislation and practice of various States in the Union to show how low the citizen may be degraded by the combined wisdom and justice of his fellow-citizens. In the early legislation of a number of the States the most humiliating punishments were denounced against persons guilty of certain crimes and misdemeanors—

the lash, the pillory, the cropping of the ears, and the branding of the face with an indelible mark of infamy. And yet a lower depth: in several of the States the common punishment of the crime of *vagrancy* was *sale into bondage at public auction!* And yet I have not read that such unfortunates thereby lost their natural-born citizenship, nor that their descendants are doomed to perpetual exclusion and degradation.

I am inclined to think that these objections, as to color and ancestral race, arise entirely from a wrong conception of the nature and qualities of citizenship, and from the loose and unguarded phraseology too often used in the discussion of the subject. I have already given, at some length, my own views of the word and the thing—citizenship. And now I will add only a few observations before drawing your attention to certain authorities upon the subject mostly relied upon by those who support the objections.

In my opinion it is a great error, and the fruitful parent of errors, to suppose that *citizens* belong exclusively to republican forms of government. English subjects are as truly citizens as we are, and we are as truly subjects as they are. Imperial France (following imperial Rome) in the text of her laws calls her people citizens.—(*Les Codes Français*, book 1, tit. 1, ch. 1, and notes.) And we have a treaty with the present Emperor of the French, stipulating for reciprocal rights in favor of the *citizens* of the two countries respectively.—(10 Stat., p. 996, art. 7.)

It is an error to suppose that citizenship is ever hereditary. It never "passes by descent." It is as original in the child as it was in his parents. It is always either born with him or given to him directly by law.

In discussing this subject it is a misleading error to fail to mark the natural and characteristic distinction between political *rights* and political *powers*. The former belong to all citizens alike, and cohere in the very name and nature of citizenship. The latter (participation in the powers of government by voting and exercising office) does not belong to all citizens alike, nor to any citizen, merely in virtue of citizenship. His *power* always depends upon extraneous facts and superadded qualifications; which facts and qualifications are common to both citizens and aliens.

In referring to the authorities commonly adduced by those who deny the citizenship of colored people, I do not pretend to cite them all, but a few only of such as I believe to be most usually relied upon.

And I will not trouble you with a detailed examination of the reasoning employed in each case, for I have already stated my own views of the principles and laws involved in the question ; and where they conflict with the arguments upon which the contrary opinion is founded, I still adhere to my own.

The first of these authorities of which I will treat is the opinion of my predecessor, Mr. Wirt, upon a case precisely like the present, except that in that case the "free person of color" was a Virginian, and the objections to his competency were founded mainly, if not entirely, upon Virginia law.—(See Opinions of Attorneys General, vol. 1, p. 506, date November 7, 1821.) I have examined this opinion with the greater care, because of the writer's reputation for learning and his known and varied excellencies as a man.

In that case the precise question was, "whether free persons of color are, *in Virginia*, citizens of the United States, within the intent and meaning of the acts regulating foreign and coasting trade, so as to be qualified to command vessels." And thus Mr. Wirt was in a manner invited to consider the question rather in a statal than a national point of view; and hence we ought not to be surprised to find the whole argument for the exclusion based upon local institutions and statal laws.

As a general answer to all such arguments, I have this to say: Every citizen of the United States is a component member of the nation, with rights and duties, under the Constitution and laws of the United States, which cannot be destroyed or abridged by the laws of any particular State. The laws of the State, if they conflict with the laws of the nation, are of no force. The Constitution is plain beyond cavil upon this point. Article 6: "This Constitution, and the laws of the United States which shall be made in pursuance thereof, and all treaties, &c., shall be the supreme law of the land, and the judges in *every State* shall be bound thereby, anything in the constitution or laws of *any State* to the contrary notwithstanding." And from this I assume that every person who is a citizen of the United States, whether by birth or naturalization, holds his great franchise by the laws of the United States, and above the control of any particular State. Citizenship of the United States is an integral thing, incapable of legal existence in fractional parts. Whoever, then, has that franchise is a whole citizen and a citizen of the whole nation, and cannot be (as the argument of my learned predecessor seems to suppose) such citizen in one State and not in another.

2

I fully concur in the statement that "the description, *citizen of the United States*, used in the Constitution, has the same meaning that it has in the several acts of Congress passed under the authority of the Constitution." And I freely declare my inability to conceive of any second or subordinate meaning of the phrase as used in all those instruments. It means in them all the simple expression of the political status of the person in connection with the nation—that he is a member of the body politic. And that is all it means, for it does not specify his rights and duties as a citizen, nor in any way refer to such "rights, privileges, and immunities" as he may happen to have, by State laws or otherwise, over and beyond what legally and naturally belong to him in his quality of citizen of the United States. State laws may and do, nay must, vest in individuals great privileges, powers, and duties which do not belong to the mass of their fellow-citizens, and in doing so they consult discretion and convenience only. One citizen, who happens to be a judge, may, under proper circumstances, sentence another to be hanged, and a third, who happens to be governor, may grant a pardon to the condemned man, who, *as a citizen*, is the undoubted peer of both the judge and the governor.

As to the objection (not in law, but sentiment only) that if a negro can be a citizen of the United States, he might, possibly, become President, the legal inference is true. There would be such a legal possibility. But those who make that objection are not arguing upon the Constitution as it is, but upon what, in their own minds and feelings, they think it ought to be. Moreover, they seem to forget that all limitations upon eligibility to office are less restrictions upon the rights of aspirants than upon the powers of electors. Even the legislature of the State, however unanimous, have no power to send to the Senate of the United States their wisest and best man, unless he be thirty years old. And all the people of the nation, speaking with one united voice, cannot, constitutionally, make any man President who happens to be under thirty-five. This is, obviously, a restriction upon the appointing power—that is, in our popular government, a restriction upon the people themselves. As individuals, we may like it or dislike it, and flatter ourselves into the belief that *we* could make a wiser and better frame of government than our fathers made. Still it is our Constitution, binding upon us and upon every citizen from the moment of birth or naturalization.

The Constitution, I suppose, says what it means, and does not mean what it does not say. It says nothing about "the high characteristic privileges of a citizen of the State" (of Virginia or any other.) I do not know what they were, but certainly in Virginia, for the first half of the existence of the commonwealth, the right of suffrage was not one of them. For during that period no man ever voted there *because* he was a free white adult male citizen. He voted on his freehold, in land; and no candidate, in soliciting his election, appealed to the people or the citizens, but to the *freeholders* only, for they alone could vote.

I shall not trouble you with any argument touching the list of disabilities declared by the laws of Virginia against free negroes and mulattoes, as stated in the opinion, because they are such only as the legislature, if so minded, might have denounced as well against a portion of its own acknowledged citizens, whose weakness might necessitate submission.

It is said in the opinion that "the allegiance which the free man of color owes to the State of Virginia is no evidence of citizenship, for he owes it not in consequence of an oath of allegiance." This proposition surprises me; perhaps I do not understand it. I did verily believe that the oath of allegiance was not the cause but the sequence of citizenship, given only as a solemn guarantee for the performance of duties already incurred. But if it be true that the oath of allegiance must either create or precede citizenship, then it follows, of necessity, that there can be no *natural-born citizen*, as the Constitution affirms, because the child must needs be born before it can take the oath.

The opinion, supported by the arguments upon which I have commented, is in these words:

"Upon the whole, I am of the opinion that free persons of color *in Virginia* are not citizens of the United States, within the intent and meaning of the acts regulating foreign and coasting trade so as to be qualified to command vessels."

As an authority this opinion is rebutted by the opinion of Attorney General Legaré, above cited.—(4 Op. A. G., 147, date March 15, 1843.) Under an act of Congress which limited the pre-emption of public land to citizens of the United States and aliens who had declared intention to become citizens, according to the naturalization laws, Mr. Legaré was of opinion that a free colored man was competent to pre-empt the land.

In that same opinion Mr. Legaré makes a just distinction between political and civil rights, which, I believe, is common to most nations.

The French code expresses it very plainly, thus: "L'exercice des droits civils est ind pendant de la qualité de *citoyen*, laquelle ne s'acquiert et ne se conserve que conformément à la loi constitutionelle."

The next authority I shall consider is a decision of the Department of State made in Mr. Marcy's time, November 4, 1856, and evidenced by a letter of that date from Mr. Thomas, Assistant Secretary, to Mr. Rice, of New York. That decision is entitled to great consideration, because upon such political questions the Secretary of State is of high authority. The case was an application for passports to travel in foreign parts, in favor of certain free blacks of some of the northern States, and the time was a few months after the passage of the act of August 18, 1856, (the first act directing the issuing of passports to individuals and restricting the issue to *citizens* of the United States, though the practice is much older.)

The letter, after stating the case, declares emphatically that "if this be so (*i. e.*, if they be negroes) there can be no doubt that they are not citizens of the United States." If this stood alone there could be no doubt of the opinion of the department at that time. But it does not stand alone. The letter, after citing several authorities, and among them one from Tennessee, to which I will have occasion to refer by name, concludes with this qualifying paragraph, which leaves some doubt as to what was the real practical opinion of Mr. Secretary Marcy at that time. The letter, assuming that a passport is a certificate of citizenship, proceeds to say:

"Such being the construction of the Constitution in regard to free persons of color, it is conceived that they cannot be regarded, *when beyond the jurisdiction of this government*, as entitled to the *full rights* of citizens, but the Secretary directs me to say that though the department could not certify that such persons are citizens of the United States, yet, if satisfied of the truth of the facts, it would give a certificate that they were *born in the United States*, are free, and that *the government thereof would regard it to be its duty* to protect them, if wronged by a foreign government, while within its jurisdiction for a legal and proper purpose."

It seems to me that the certificate proposed to be given would be, in substance and fact, a good passport, for the act of Congress prescribes no form for the passport, and requires no particular fact to appear upon its face. And I confidently believe that there is not a government in Europe which, in view of our laws of citizenship, would question the validity of a passport which declares upon its face that the bearer is *a free natural-born inhabitant of the United States.*

I turn now to the consideration of the Tennessee case, referred to and relied upon in the letter from the State Department—the State of Tennessee *vs.* Ambrose, (1 Meig's R., 331,) adjudged in 1838. Ambrose, being a free negro emancipated in Kentucky, moved to and settled in Tennessee. He was indicted for that crime against the Tennessee statute, made to prevent the ingress of that sort of people. He demurred to the indictment upon the ground that he was a citizen of Kentucky, and as such had a right under the Constitution of the United States (art. 4, sec. 2) to go to and abide in Tennessee in spite of the State statute. The court in which the indictment was found sustained the demurrer. The public prosecutor took the case up to the supreme court, where the judgment below was reversed, and it was held by the court that Ambrose, under the circumstances, could not be a citizen of Kentucky, and therefore could not claim the protection of the national Constitution as against the Tennessee statute.

I must trouble you with a few remarks upon certain passages in the opinion of the court, which constitute the foundation of the judgment, and without which the judgement itself, having no legal basis to rest upon, ought not to have any authority as a precedent.

The court, after stating the case and citing from the Constitution, (art. 4. sec. 2) "the citizens *of* each State shall be entitled to all the privileges and immunities of citizens *in* the several States," proceeds: "the citizens here spoken of (says the supreme court of Tennessee) are those who are entitled to '*all* the privileges and immunities of citizens.' But free negroes, by whatever appellation we call them, were never *in any of the States* entitled to *all* the privileges and immunities of citizens, and consequently were not intended to be included when this word was used in the Constitution.

"In this country," (continues the court,) "under the free government created by the Constitution, whose language we are expounding, the humblest *white* citizen is entitled to *all* 'the privileges and immunities' which the *most exalted one enjoys.* Hence, in speaking of the rights which a citizen of one State shall enjoy in every other State, as applicable to *white men,* it is very properly said that he should be entitled to *all* the privileges and immunities of citizens in each other State. The meaning of the language is that no privilege enjoyed by, or immunity allowed to, the most favored class of citizens in said State shall be withheld from a citizen of any other State. How can it be said that he enjoys *all* the *privileges*, when he is scarcely allowed a *single right* in common with the mass of the citizens of the State?

"It cannot be; and therefore either the free negro is not a citizen, in the sense of the Constitution, or, if a citizen, he is entitled to 'all the privileges and immunities' of the *most favored class of citizens.* But this latter consequence will be contended by no one. It must then follow that they are not citizens."

These are the foundations of the judgment in the case of Ambrose, and not only in that but in almost every similar case which I have had occasion to examine. A good deal of what I have already said is strictly applicable here, and in trying to show the fallacy of the reasoning of the court in Tennessee, I must take the risk of some needless repetition.

The leading thought, that indeed which seems to have compelled the judgment against Ambrose, is, in my opinion, a naked assumption, not supported by any word of written law, nor maintainable by logical argument. It is assumed that a person to be a citizen at all *must* have *all* the rights, privileges, and immunities which the most *favored one* enjoys; all of the most *favored class* of citizens. Now, if there be grades and classes of citizens, (which I am not exactly willing to admit,) it would seem that there must be something to distinguish the grades; some difference in the rights, privileges, and immunities of the different classes. And yet the court, while asserting the existence of different classes of citizens, asserts also their equality, by declaring that "*the humblest* white citizen is entitled to *all* the 'privileges and immunities' which the *most exalted* one enjoys." Then what marks the difference of classes? By what line can we separate humility from exaltation, as applied to a citizen?

In fact, it seems to me that the difficulties which surround the subject are artificial, created by the habitual confounding of things different in their nature and origin, and by the persistent abuse of language. No distinction is drawn between the rights and duties of a man as a citizen and his rights and duties as a member of society, without regard to his citizenship. The first are political merely—the last civil and social only. And the words *rights*, *privileges*, *immunities* are abusively used, as if they were synonymous. The word *rights* is generic, common, embracing whatever may be lawfully claimed. *Privileges* are special rights belonging to the individual or class, and not to the mass. *Immunities* are rights of exemption only—freedom from what otherwise would be a duty, obligation, or burden. For instance, the constitution of Tennessee (art. 4, sec. 1) declares that "all free men of color shall be exempt from military duty, *in time of peace*, and also from paying a free poll-tax." This is an immunity.

But whether there be or be not grades and classes of citizens, higher or lower, more or less favored, is wholly immaterial to this question. For the Constitution speaks of *citizens* only, without any reference to their rank, grade, or class, or to the number or magnitude of their rights, privileges, and immunities—*citizens* simply, without an adjective to qualify, enlarge, or diminish their rights and capacities. Therefore, if there be grades and classes of citizens, still the lowest individual of the lowest possible class is a citizen, and as such fills the requirement of the Constitution.

If we must have grades and classes of citizens, higher and lower, more and less favored, it seems to me impossible to sustain the proposition of the court that the humblest and the most exalted are entitled to equal privileges and immunities. A free, white, natural-born female infant is certainly a citizen, and I suppose it would be but reasonable to place her in the lowest class. And I assume that it would not be deemed unreasonable to call that class the highest out of which the President must be chosen. If eligibility to the presidency be a *privilege* in the lawful candidate—a peculiar right belonging to him, and not to the mass of citizens, then there *is* some difference; *she* is not entitled to *all* his privileges.

Those who most indulge in the assumption that to constitute a citizen at all the person must have all the privileges and immunities which any citizen can enjoy, rarely venture to specify precisely what they mean. Generally, I think, the inference is plain that they mean suffrage and eligibility; and, in that connection, I think I have already shown that suffrage and eligibility have no necessary connection with citizenship, and that the one may, and often does, exist without the other.

Again, "immunities" are enjoyed to a very large extent by free negroes in all the slaveholding States. They are generally exempted by law from the onerous duties of jurors in the courts, and militia men in the field; and these are immunities eagerly desired by many white men in all the States.

In another part of that opinion, the court declares that the word "freemen," as used in the constitution of Tennessee, is equivalent to *citizen;* and yet the court denies that the phrase "freemen of color," used in the same constitution, is a proper designation of citizens! I close my remarks upon that case with an extract from the constitution of Tennessee, (which was originally made in 1795, and amended in 1835,) reminding you only that, until 1790, Tennessee was a part of North Carolina, and subject to its constitution and laws, and hence the peculiar phraseology of the extract:

"Article 4, section 1. Every free white man, of the age of twenty-one years, being a citizen of the *United States* and a citizen of the *county* wherein he may offer his vote six months next preceding the day of election, shall be entitled to vote for members of the general assembly and other civil officers for the county or district in which he resides: *Provided*, that no person shall be disqualified for voting, in any election, *on account of color*, who is now, by the laws of this State, a competent witness in a court of justice against a white man. All freemen of color shall be exempt from military duty in time of peace, and also from paying a free poll-tax."

Finally, the celebrated case of Scott *vs.* Sanford, 19 Howard's Reports, 393, is sometimes cited as a direct authority against the capacity of free persons of color to be citizens of the United States. That is an entire mistake. The case, as it stands of record, does not determine, nor purport to determine, that question. It was an ordinary suit for freedom, very common in our jurisprudence, and especially provided for in the legislation of most of the slaveholding States, as it is in Missouri. For convenience the form of the action usually is (and is in this case) *trespass*, alleging an assault and battery and false imprisonment, so as to enable the defendant, (the master,) if he choose, to make a direct issue upon the freedom or slavery of the plaintiff, which is the real point and object of the action, by pleading, in justification of the alleged trespass, that the plaintiff is a slave—his own or another man's.

Such an action Dred Scott, if entitled to freedom, might have brought in the State court, without any allegation of citizenship, and without being, in fact, a citizen. But it seems he desired to bring his action in the circuit court of the United States in Missouri; and, to enable him to do that, he had to allege citizenship, because Mr. Sandford, the defendant, was a citizen of New York, and unless the plaintiff were a citizen of Missouri (or some other State) the national court had no jurisdiction of the case.

The plaintiff having made his election to sue in the United States court, the defendant might, if he would, have pleaded *in bar* to the merits of the action, but he exercised his election to plead *in abate-*

ment to the jurisdiction of the court; thus, that the action, if any, "accrued to the said Dred Scott out of the jurisdiction of this court, and exclusively within the jurisdiction of the courts of the State of Missouri, for that, to wit, the said plaintiff, Dred Scott, is not a citizen of the State of Missouri, as alleged in his declaration, [not because he was not born there, and born free, but] *because he is a negro* of African descent; his ancestors were of pure African blood, and were brought into this country and sold as negro slaves, and this the said Sandford is ready to verify. Wherefore he prays judgment whether this court can or will take further cognizance of the action aforesaid." To this plea the plaintiff demurred, and the circuit court sustained the demurrer, thereby declaring that the facts stated in the plea, and confessed by the demurrer, did not disqualify Scott for being a citizen of Missouri, and so that the United States circuit court had jurisdiction of the cause.

The circuit court having taken jurisdiction, the defendant had, of course, to *plead over* to the merits of the action. He did so, and issues were joined, and there was an elaborate trial of the facts, which resulted in a verdict and judgment in favor of the defendant. And thereupon the plaintiff brought the case up to the Supreme Court by writ of error.

The power of the Supreme Court over the proceedings and judgments of the circuit court is appellate only, and this for the sole purpose of enabling the court above to affirm what has been rightly done, and reverse what has been wrongly done in the court below. If the error of the court below consist in the illegal assumption of power to hear and determine the merits of a case not within its jurisdiction, of course the court above will correct that error, by setting aside whatever may have been done by that usurped authority. And in doing this the court above has no more power than the court below had to hear and determine the merits of the case. And to assume the power to determine a case not within the jurisdiction is as great an error in the court above as in the court below; for it is equally true, in all courts, that the jurisdiction must first be ascertained before proceeding to judgment.

In this particular case the Supreme Court did first examine and consider the plea in abatement, and did adjudge that it was a good plea, sufficient to oust the jurisdiction of the circuit court. And hence it follows, as a necessary legal consequence, that whatever was done in the circuit court after the plea in abatement, and touching

UofM

the merits of the case, was simply void, because done *coram non judice.*

Pleas in abatement were never favorites with the courts in England or America. Lord Coke tells us that they must be "certain to a certain intent, in every particular," and in practice they are always dealt with very strictly. When, therefore, the Supreme Court affirmed the plea in abatement in this case, I assume that it is affirmed, in manner and form, as written, and not otherwise. And this not merely because pleas in abatement are always considered *stricti legis*, but also, and chiefly, because the decision tends to abridge the valuable rights of persons natural-born in the country, which rights ought not to be impaired, except upon the clearest evidence of fact and law.

Taking the plea, then, strictly as it is written, the persons who are excluded by this judgment from being citizens of Missouri must be negroes, not mulattoes nor mestizos, nor quadroons. They must be of *African* descent, not Asiatic, even though they come of the blackest Malays in southeastern Asia. They must have had *ancestors*, (yet that may be doubtful, if born in slavery, of putative parents, who were slaves, and being slaves, incapable of contracting matrimony, and therefore every child must needs be a bastard, and so, by the common law, *nullius filius*, and incapable of ancestors.) His ancestors, if he had any, must have been of *pure* African blood, not mixed with the tawny Moor of Morocco or the dusky Arab of the desert, both of whom had their origin in Asia. They must have been *brought* to this country, not come voluntarily; and *sold*, not kept by the importer for his own use, nor given to his friends.

In this argument I raise no question upon the legal validity of the judgment in Scott *vs.* Sandford. I only insist that the judgment in that case is limited in law, as it is, in fact, limited on the face of the record, to the plea in abatement; and, consequently, that whatever was said in the long course of the case, as reported, (240 pages,) respecting the legal merits of the case, and respecting any supposed legal disability resulting from the mere fact of color, though entitled to all the respect which is due to the learned and upright sources from which the opinions come, was "*dehors the record*," and of no authority as a judicial decision.

To show that, notwithstanding all that was *said* upon other subjects, the *action* of the court was strictly confined to the plea in abatement, I copy the judgment:

"Upon the whole, therefore, it is the judgment of this court that it appears by the record before us that the plaintiff in error is not a citizen of Missouri, *in the sense in which that word is used in the Constitution*, and that the circuit court of the United States, for that reason, *had no jurisdiction in the case, and could give no judgment in it.* Its judgment for the defendant must, consequently, be reversed, and a mandate issued, directing the suit to be *dismissed for want of jurisdiction.*"

And now, upon the whole matter, I give it as my opinion that the *free man of color*, mentioned in your letter, if born in the United States, is a citizen of the United States, and, if otherwise qualified, is competent, according to the acts of Congress, to be master of a vessel engaged in the coasting trade.

All of which is respectfully submitted by your obedient servant,

EDWARD BATES,

Attorney General.

www.ingramcontent.com/pod-product-compliance
Lightning Source LLC
LaVergne TN
LVHW011139110826
845150LV00008B/2403
* 9 7 8 1 4 1 8 1 9 3 1 9 5 *